Understanding...

I Know Someone with Autism

Sue Barraclough

Raintree

www.raintreepublishers.co.uk
Visit our website to find out
more information about
Raintree books.

To order:
☎ Phone 0845 6044371
🖹 Fax +44 (0) 1865 312263
🖾 Email myorders@raintreepublishers.co.uk

Customers from outside the UK please telephone +44 1865 312262

Raintree is an imprint of Capstone Global Library Limited,
a company incorporated in England and Wales having
its registered office at 7 Pilgrim Street, London, EC4V 6LB –
Registered company number: 6695582

Text © Capstone Global Library Limited 2011
First published in hardback in 2011
First published in paperback in 2012
The moral rights of the proprietor have been asserted.

Edited by Rebecca Rissman, Daniel Nunn
    and Siân Smith
Designed by Joanna Hinton Malivoire
Picture research by Mica Brancic
Originated by Capstone Global Library
Printed and bound in China by Leo Paper Products Ltd

ISBN 978 1 406 22074 2 (hardback)
15 14 13 12 11
10 9 8 7 6 5 4 3 2 1

ISBN 978 1 406 22347 7 (paperback)
16 15 14 13 12 11
10 9 8 7 6 5 4 3 2 1

British Library Cataloguing in Publication Data
Barraclough, Sue.
  I know someone with autism. – (Understanding health
issues)
  1. Autism–Juvenile literature.
  I. Title II. Series
  616.8'5882-dc22

Acknowledgements
We would like to thank the following for permission to
reproduce photographs: Alamy p. 22 (© Lyndsay Russell);
Corbis p. 16 (© Grady Reese); Getty Images pp. 12
(PhotoAlto/Eric Audras), 13 (Dorling Kindersley/Andy
Crawford), 14 (Photographer's Choice/Mieke Dalle), 23
(Fuse), 25 (Tetra Images), 26 (Wirelmage/John Shearer);
iStockphoto pp. 4 left (© Eileen Hart), 14 (© Chris Schmidt);
Photolibrary pp. 5 (BSIP Medical/Laurent/Helen), 6
(Brand X Pictures), 8 (Juice Images), 15 (Paul Doyle), 19
(Flirt Collection/Michael Prince), 20 (Alexis Maryon), 21
(imagebroker.net/Michael Peuckert), 24 (Tetra Images/
Jetta Productions/Walter Hodges); Rex Features p. 27
(Everett Collection); Shutterstock pp. 4 right (© Adrian
Hughes), 11 (© John McLaird), 17 (© Igor Kisselev), 18 (©
Yevgen Kotyukh).

Cover photograph of a boy working on a pottery wheel
reproduced with permission of Getty Images (The Image
Bank/John Kelly).

We would like to thank Matthew Siegel and Ashley Wolinski
for their invaluable help in the preparation of this book.

Contents

Some words are printed in bold, **like this**. You can find out what they mean in the glossary.

Do you know someone with autism?

Do you have any friends who have autism? Some people with autism cannot **communicate** well. They may find it hard to understand other people and what they mean.

Some people with autism may not realize that a smile can mean someone feels happy, and a frown can mean that they feel sad.

Being in a new place can be difficult for a person with autism.

Some people with autism can be upset by changes. Many people do not like change, but this does not mean they are autistic. Someone with autism may find change very worrying or even scary.

What is autism?

Autism is a **condition** that affects how people see and act with the world. There are many different types and levels of autism. This is known as the **autistic spectrum**.

Some people who have autism like to do daily tasks such as washing up, or going to bed in exactly the same way.

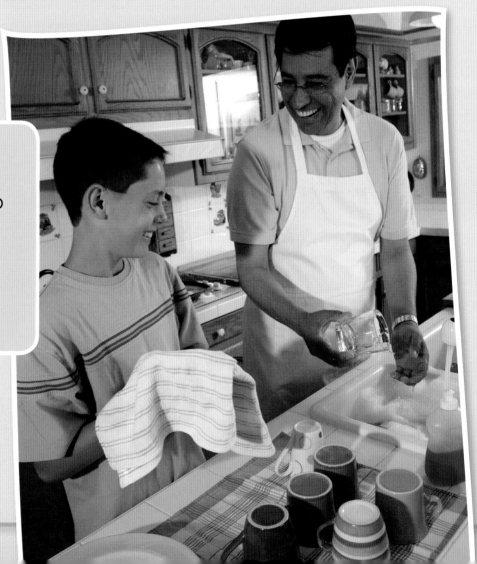

Every person with autism is different. Some people with autism never learn to talk. Some people have such mild autism that they never even know that they have it.

Having autism can mean:

- hating change and liking **routines**
- not liking to meet new people or do new activities
- avoiding **eye contact**
- saying the same thing or doing the same thing over and over
- focussing on one object or one activity.

What causes autism?

Nobody is really sure what causes autism. Autism may be **genetic**. This means it is passed from parents to their children. It is not possible to catch autism from another person.

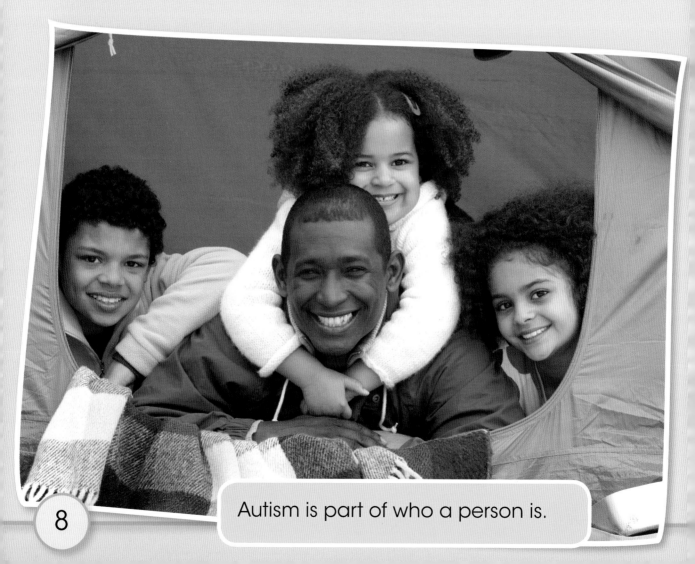

Autism is part of who a person is.

Certain parts of the brain control different activities such as moving, feeling, thinking, and talking. Scientists think that parts of the brain develop differently in a person who has autism.

touch

movement

sight

speech

behaviour and feelings

hearing

This picture shows just a few of the things controlled by different parts of our brains.

Understanding autism

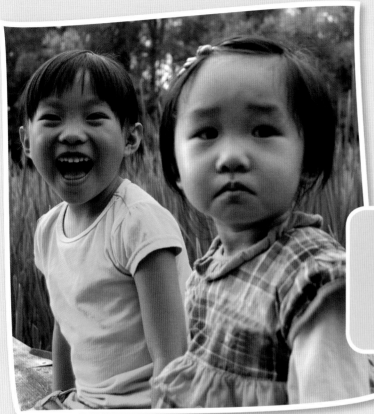

Someone with autism may not understand that somebody else feels happy or upset.

Some people with autism find it hard to understand how other people feel. For example, they might laugh if someone is hurt. They are not being mean, they just do not understand how other people feel.

Many people with autism move differently. A person with autism may rock, flap their hands, jump up and down, or make faces. Movements like this make a person with autism feel safe and in control.

Repeating movements sometimes helps people with autism to let out their feelings.

Feelings about change

Some people with autism like to do things in a certain way. They might get angry or upset if a **routine** is changed. A routine makes them feel safe and in control.

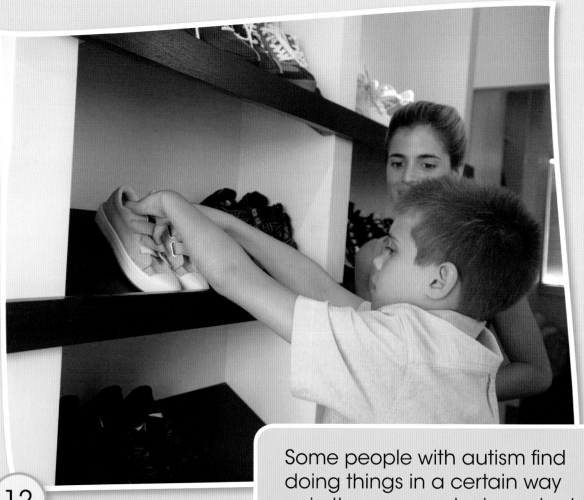

Some people with autism find doing things in a certain way or in the same order important.

A person with autism may like things to stay the same. They might get upset if things are moved.

Some people with autism find changes or having to do new things very worrying. It can help if they know about changes that are going to happen. It is important for others to understand that change can be difficult for someone with autism.

Communication

People need to pass information on to each other all the time. This is called **communication**. Many people with autism need help to communicate better. They may need to learn simple skills such as making **eye contact**.

If you look at someone while they are talking it helps to show them that you are listening.

We can learn lots of different ways to communicate.

Having support at an early age can help many children with autism to learn to talk. Some people with autism are not able to talk but learn **sign language** or use pictures to communicate.

Some people have a form of autism called **Asperger's**. Many people with Asperger's can learn and **communicate** well but they have problems with **social skills**. These skills are to do with how we understand others and make friends.

People with Asperger's can have difficulty understanding what people mean or how they feel.

Someone with autism may be more sensitive to loud noises.

Many people with autism need special help because they experience the world differently. For someone with autism sights, smells, or sounds can be very strong.

Strengths and support

Many people with autism can have special strengths and talents. For example, they may be able to play a piece of music after only hearing it once, or be able to remember long lists of information.

Some people with autism are very talented artists.

Everyone has different strengths and weaknesses. Each person with autism can find different things they can do well and needs different kinds of help.

Different people enjoy doing different things.

Living with autism

Special teachers and carers give support with learning different skills.

There is no **cure** for autism but people can learn ways to overcome some of the difficulties they have. People with autism can learn new skills that will help them in the future. They can find ways of controlling difficult behaviours.

It is important that children with autism get help and support as early as possible. People with autism can often learn to be independent and go on to have jobs and families of their own.

This woman worked hard to become a vet.

Being a good friend

Autism affects people differently. Some people with autism hate to be touched, and some love to be hugged tightly. Some people with autism hate bright colours, and some love them. Some people with autism enjoy loud noises, but some find them scary.

Good friends understand each other.

You can help by understanding that a friend with autism may not want to join in games and other group activities.

You can be a good friend by learning about the things your friend likes and how they want to be treated. A person with autism often likes places that are quiet and familiar. You can help by making sure your friend feels safe.

How can I help?

Someone with autism may not always understand some words or phrases. For example if you said that you "laughed your head off" they might find it scary. You can help a friend with autism by speaking plainly and simply.

If a friend finds something difficult to understand, try to explain it in a different way.

You can help a friend with autism to learn and discover things they can do well.

Some people with autism are very good at subjects such as maths, art, and music. They can also be very good at concentrating on one activity. This often means they can learn to do it very well.

Famous people with autism

Jason McElwain found out he had autism when he was young, and struggled to make friends at school. He worked hard to improve his **social skills** and got involved with the school basketball team. Jason now helps to raise money for autism research.

Jason McElwain became famous when he played for 4 minutes at the end of a basketball match and scored 20 points.

One of the most famous of Daryl Hannah's films is about a mermaid who is found washed up on a beach.

Daryl Hannah's parents were told she was borderline autistic when she was very young. She later became an actress and has starred in many successful films.

Autism – true or false?

People with autism are unfriendly. They do not want to make friends.

FALSE! People with autism want to have friends but they sometimes find it difficult to talk to strangers and are not sure how to act.

There are four times as many boys with autism than girls.

TRUE! More boys than girls have autism.

You cannot catch autism from another person.

TRUE! It is not possible to catch autism from someone else.

It is the parents' fault that children have autism. A child with autism is just behaving badly.

FALSE! Autism has nothing to do with the way a child is brought up. A child with autism cannot help behaving differently.

Glossary

Asperger's type of autism where a person has difficulties with social skills and finds it hard to understand how people feel

autistic spectrum name for the wide range of different types and levels of autism

communicate pass information on

condition something that affects the way some parts of the body work

cure medical treatment that makes someone better

eye contact looking into someone's eyes

genetic something which is passed on from parents to their children

routine set order for doing things

sign language way of communicating using hands and fingers

social skills skills used for understanding people and making friends

Find out more

Books to read

A Book About What Autism Can Be Like, Sue Adams (Jessica Kingsley Publishers, 2009)

Everybody is Different, Fiona Bleach (Autism Asperger Publishing, 2002)

My Sister is Different, Sarah Tamsin Hunter (National Autistic Society, 2006)

Websites

www.autism.org.uk
The National Autistic Society website has lots of information on autism and Asperger's along with links to other useful organisations.

www.cyh.com
Click on the 'Kids' Health' button and then search for 'Autism' to discover more about Autism and Asperger's.

Index